REFINEMENT OF CHARACTER

I0165296

REFINEMENT OF CHARACTER

Friday Discourses
by Shaykh Fadhlalla Haeri

Zahra Publications

The author would like to thank Sajida Ismail,
Almas Nanabhay, Saadiya Khan, Yunus Ismail,
Yacoob Moosa, Haider Mahdi, Ahmed Sheriff,
Laa'iqah SeedSower and Leyya Kalla
for their assistance in bringing this booklet
into production.

First published in 2015

Distributed & Re-published in 2018

Publisher: Zahra Publications

www.sfhfoundation.com

www.zahrapublications.com

© Shaykh Fadhlalla Haeri, 2018

Designed and typeset in South Africa by
Quintessence Publishing

Cover Design by Mizpah Marketing Concepts

Set in 11 point on 14 point, Garamond

Printed and bound by Lightning Source

ISBN (Printed Version) – Paperback: 978-1-928329-05-3

Table of Contents

Introduction

"How do we transform ourselves using the spiritual map from our *Din*? How do we move through the four stages of inner awakening from *Ilma Al Yaqin* (the Total Reality of Certainty) to *Ayn Al-Yaqin* (the Eye of certainty) to *Haqq Al-Yaqin* (the Total Reality of Certainty) and its final stage, *Haqq Al-Haqq* (the Truth of Truth).

What is the Quranic prescription of life, which allows the refinement of character from base to sublime? How do your temporal desires, your *nafs*, your ego and your *fitrah* resonate with the sub-lime Infinite? How does modern-day personality pigeon-holing, such as the Myers Briggs Type Indicator completely distort the true inner person?

There is a better way to seek the truth from the inside out, rather than the outside in.

Our Prophet showed us the way, both for *Din* and *Dunya*. His outward habits and *adab* were exemplary and his inner *sunnah* was his compass.

So how does one move up from the base; **The Comanding Self** – *Nafs* **al amarra**, to the slightly higher **Blaming Self** – *Nafs* **al-lawwama**, to the improved **Inspired Self** – *Nafs* **al-mulhama** and finally to the now under control *nafs* **The Certain Self** – *Nafs* **al-mutma'inna**?

How do we nurture better relationships with others and realise that there is no otherness and the only relationship is with the *ruh*, with Allah and His Light. The Self is also ever-present in its three forms. At the base is The Vegetal Self, focussed on food, growth and reproduction. Then, the Animal Self, with additional powers of movement and comprehension and finally The Rational Self, with power of action and knowledge with discernment.

We must understand the cosmic evolution and creational map from the Alam-i-Hahut (Realm of Oneness) and pre-existence to the Alam-i-Malakut (Angelic Realm and separate consciousness) and finally to our current state of Alam-i-Nasut (Realm of humans and the tangible world of matter). From the indescribable ones of *Hahut* to the earthiness of *Mulk*, such is His Design.

Each Self fluctuates from virtue to vice, one interplaying with the other and finally balance – for the ultimate joy is to die before one dies – from moving away from that which is not acceptable (*Hijrah*), to intent and *Jihad* of expending energy to *Amal*, action. It is in understanding these that we achieve Oneness with our Original source. Light upon Lights"

Haider Mahdi

The 'Refinement of Character' discourses present a comprehensive and complete package of essentials regarding the self and its emergence, of the interplay between the ego and the soul (behaviour and personality dynamics). With reflection on the discourses, one comes closer to discovering the true answers for these questions:

☼ What is the human character?

☼ What is personality?

☼ What is behaviour?

☼ What is the relationship between the mind and behaviour?

Self and Soul Interplay

"The most challenging issue in human existence is to understand the nature of the self. Some of the most frequently asked questions are 'Who am I?', and 'What can I do to be content and happy?' Some people are naturally endowed with a healthy disposition from early on in life and seem to attract positive outcomes. For others, a better knowledge of the relationship between one's ego and the higher self is necessary. Life and its quality are related to the extent of our ability to refer to higher a consciousness within ourselves."

Shaykh Fadhlalla Haeri,
Pointers to Presence

In several former communities, change of behaviour caused change of mind. Parents, extended family and society would say 'Do this', 'Be generous', 'Be correct', 'Sit still' and the mind changed. Nowadays we use remedies and interferences which we bring into our system, to influence the mind and then hopefully behaviour.

Psychiatry developed its own systems of *personality evaluation* in order to attempt answering the questions 'What is behaviour?', 'What is personality?' and 'How can we bring about changes that are appropriate?'

Most of us who have religious sentiments, respect for the *Din*, the Qur'an and the way of the Prophet see the *Din* as 'out there', and not 'here and now'. If we want to revive ourselves, we must make the teachings immediately usable, important and urgent so that it becomes information which leads to transformation. And, the first people who need to live, enjoy and be illumined by their *Din* are ourselves.

The teachings of Sufism talk about four stages of inner awakening or *Certainty*:

☼ *Ilm al-yaqin* (the *knowledge* of Certainty). *Ilm al-yaqin* is a mental and intellectual understanding, or appreciation of an experience e.g. having the *knowledge* of something called fire or water or something called honey.

☼ *The second stage is called ayn al-yaqin (the eye of Certainty). This is the stage of witnessing. You see the fire, water and honey.*

☼ *The next stage is haqq al-yaqin (the total reality of Certainty) which is when you undergo an actual interactive experience e.g. have actually tasted the water, tasted the honey or touched the fire.*

☼ *The last stage is haqq al-haqq (the Truth of Truth). Now there is no longer a duality between experiencer and experienced. You are consumed by the fire, water or honey; you are engulfed by it and transformed by it. You have no doubt what it is, what goodness is, what wrongdoing is or what a lie is.*

So, you start with knowledge, then move to perception and then towards truly experiencing it. This is the reason why, if information does not lead to transformation, it is gone; because you have not connected with it. When you hear a true teaching, it should move you to immediately act upon it. If you do not act, you have missed it.

Preaching is less and less popular due to the fact that the information received has not moved the heart. And yet, our *Din* has it all to move us into the transformative zone without changing anything in our lives except the manner in which we respond to events and circumstances.

In terms of *refinement of character*, consider The Qur'an's description of the quality of the character of the Prophet Muhammad:

> *'And indeed, you are of a great moral character.' [68:4]*

The notion of the complete human being or the *Insan al-kamil* was addressed by early Islamic scholars and masters from the model of the Prophet and his exemplary conduct. Prophets, sages, imams and sufi masters have elaborated upon a life fulfilled by enlightenment and God-realisation. This experience is the outcome of leaving behind self-illusion, identity and duality.

How does one complete one's character and bring it to its full refinement? It is by turning away from the lower self! It is by the suffering of the lower self from its vices and negative traits. It is by turning to the higher and positive qualities.

What is refinement? How can we change and perfect our character?

Allah reminds us in the Qur'an:

'We have certainly created man in the best of stature.' [95:4]

Allah has created *insan*, the complete human being, and has illustrated the full story of the human being, in the best and most perfect way.

'Then We return him to the lowest of the low' [95:5]

We can sink to the lowest of the lowest, to become worse than animals.

'Except for those who believe and do righteous deeds' [95:6]

So, the Qur'an teaches us that you can maintain upward progress if you increase your faith and trust, and act appropriately. To act in appropriateness means to act selflessly, as though you are going to die at any moment, giving up what you treasure most – wealth and time.

Give what you love most and you will see

wonder upon wonder!

The refinement of character, moving from the lower self to the higher self, is cyclical e.g. a five year old child *has* to be selfish and egotistic but a fifty year old man with similar traits may have missed the opportunity. You have to *realise* the refinement of character in order to discover the light within the heart. It is not easy; it is like swimming against the current.

In attempting to groom young people we should remember the Quranic revelation that all entities in existence have an easy program to follow:

> *'Allah is He who has created seven heavens, and like them of the earth. Through them flows His will, so that you might come to know that Allah has the power to will anything, and that Allah encompasses all things with His knowledge' [65:12]*

We too, as human beings, have an easy programme if we follow our *fitrah*. Allah describes in the Qur'an:

> *'So direct your face toward the religion, inclining to truth. [Adhere to] the fitrah of*

Allah upon which He has created [all] people.
No change should there be in the creation of
Allah. That is the correct religion, but most of
the people do not know' [30:30].

We all have been endowed with *the code, the software* or the inner program. As a child you pursue exercising the five outer senses. In your teens, at the beginning of maturity, you begin to wonder about the five inner senses, which are far more important. The outer senses are connectors which bring you images. If these images are not properly interpreted, then we will not grow from the outer to the inner. We need to realise that each one of us contain both the outer and the inner.

Allah has created a wondrous crucible of space and time that contains us all:

'He is the First and the Last, the Ascendant
and the Intimate, and He is, of all things,
Knowing' [57:3]

This is the alchemical laboratory in which we, who think 'we are this' and 'we are that', will come to know that we are *all* and *none* of these! You certainly are the human being you think you are — born with an identity, biography and history. But is this all? If this is all, why are you not happy forever?

Yet, in a sacred tradition, Allah reveals to the Prophet that 'I have created you for eternal happiness.'

Refinement of character involves constant awareness of the purpose of life. The purpose of life is to know the qualities and the great attributes of the Life-Giver. Otherwise, you identify just with the body and one day the body is going to die. The body is a bag of sickness. There are more bacteria in the body than there are cells (estimated around 100 trillion). So, we must put things into perspective. You do not have hundreds of years, time is short.

If by the age of 40 you are not challenged by life and its purpose and meaning, then it may be too late. By the age of 50 and 60 you should know that the purpose of being in this world is to adore Allah:

> *'And I did not create the jinn and mankind except to worship Me.'* *[51:56]*

How can you worship if you do not know

the Divine qualities? Know that you worship Allah, who is al-Azim (The Magnificent), al-Qawi (The Most Strong), al-Baqi (The Everlasting), al-Awwal (The First), al-Akhir (The Last), al-Ghani (The Rich Beyond Need).

We love wealth because Allah is *al-Ghani*. Once you realise His light is in your heart, you come to know that true wealth lies in your heart. Regarding outer wealth, you and others have to chase after it. And what a struggle it is to get it, save it and keep it!

We all love freedom and emancipation. But, what freedom and emancipation are we looking for? Everybody talks about 'liberation' and 'liberty'. Rather, liberate yourself from your-self! Free yourself from the lower self! Only then can you talk about the source of freedom.

The Prophet talks about our need for three essentials only: sufficient food to reduce or put an end to the pain of hunger, clothing for the elements and shelter. If you pursue more than these, then, as you all know, trouble is upon you. The roof will leak the car will be stolen…it never ends.

Are you spending your life and energy

chasing the *dunya*? What for?

You seek contentment! Why can you not be content now? Imam Ali said that *zuhd* or asceticism does not mean you should not own anything. It means nothing should own you.

Who are you? How can you achieve what you hope and want, *now*?

By doing your *wudu*!

Close the connection with the outer world, enter your inner domain and disappear from anything that moves. Only then will you begin to get closer to that which is within. This is our *fitrah*!

Allah describes the great prophetic knowledge:

> *'Except for He who created me; and indeed, He will guide me'. [43:27]*

Another word in the Qur'an similar to *fitrah* is *taba'*. The Qur'an uses this word only in one context. *Taba'* in Arabic is to print, to press, to re-produce. *Matba'a* is a printing press.

It is Allah who has cracked you, brought you from nowhere and placed the *ruh* in your heart. Therefore you will be guided by the same Light.

The *insan* is made of the following elements – bones, muscles, a nervous system, a brain and a mind. Apart from the body, there is also the complexity of *nafs*:

> *'And [by] the soul and He who proportioned it and inspired it [with discernment of] its wickedness and its righteousness.' [91:7-8]*

The *nafs* contain the different entities (the mind, the heart and the soul or the *ruh*) and can establish *taqwa* i.e. a cautious or fearful awareness that you may leave this world at any moment.

Are you ready and happy to leave this world?

The Prophetic teaching is that *'you leave this world as your state is.'* Your starting point of life after death is 'as you have left this world.' If you are ready to leave, then you are also ready to stay because you render your personal accounts at all times.

Let us talk about the nature of the human being, the human composition and the interplay between nature and nurture.

What role does DNA play?

How important is the environment?

Is it a mixture of both that determines the

nature of the human being?

We are material, mental and spiritual. This is the composition of the human being. We also need to fine-tune our behaviour and personality. The knowledge of various stages and spiritual stations is imperative. Our heritage has wonderful traditions of *manazil-u sa'ireen* (stations of the seekers) which are the different steps of the journey.

Refinement of Character

The refinement of the self or the refinement of character involves multitudes of stages. We have already described the basic foundations of reaching the rational, accountable self by being aware – 'What are you doing?', 'Why are you doing it?', 'Will your higher self or *ruh* approve it?'

Going back two thousand years or more, before the so-called Gregorian or Christian era, we find attempts to classify personalities. When we say he is an evil character' it implies that we have *fixed* the character of the person. It is better to say that this is an *evil act*, or this is a *friendly act*, or this is an *appropriate act*, because, how do you know that this 'evil being' will not change?

This attempt to pigeon-hole personality types has been with us for thousands of years.

Thirty to forty years ago the following two types of personalities became fashionable: A-type and B-type. An A-type personality indicates an outgoing, extrovert, friendly, joyful being, and the B-type personality indicates an inward-looking, shy, laid-back and less pro-active type.

The attempt to fix things is part of every endeavour in life. We want to define it. We also want to define Allah, which is impossible. The Prophet Muhammad taught us to discuss Allah's qualities, Allah's attributes and never to discuss The Absolute Essence of Allah, as it is beyond the human being and its relative mind to discuss The Source.

In Islam we have the privilege and advantage to discuss Allah's attributes and yearn for its embodiment in our lives.

There are two aspects in us. One aspect is *the animal* which fends for itself (and human beings sometimes become worse than the animals). It is a basic evolutionary stage because it is *conditioned consciousness*. The other aspect is *the higher one* in us which, as we develop and refine, affects us more. When you are no longer prompted by *the* money you have made or the power you have you now yearn for higher qualities viz. the attributes of Allah. Allah is the Generous! We love to emulate these perfect qualities. In the Qur'an Allah calls them *sibghatullah*, the colours of Allah.

We have the glorious role models of the prophets, especially the Prophet Muhammad, which transcends all of these trends to attempt to *fix* our personality and character.

The Greek classics had four types of characters and we find the same in Eastern practices such as *Ayurveda*. The Greeks classified the characters as irritable, depressed, optimistic and calm (these are my translations). The classifications are again attempts to pigeon-hole personalities or characters.

Scientists tried to find the correlation between the shape of the body and its character or personality. These are pigeon-holed into three types – plump, muscular and lean. In the last thirty to forty years of research, modern psychology and psychiatry recognised that the Jungian 'essential four classes' of psychological types were precursors to the subsequent 'sixteen sub-types'.

I will stop using the word 'type' and will

instead use the word 'trait' because there is no fixed type. The sixteen traits follow the eight opposites or reflective qualities – extroversion, introversion, intuitive, sensing, thinking, feeling, judgmental and perceiving.

Let us look at an analogy – a desired executive in a company has the following four main characteristics: extroversion (E), intuitiveness (I) or looking ahead to the future, thinking (T) and not just following his feelings or his emotions and then judging (J) rather than waiting until it is too late. The EITJ is considered a good combination. There are many books written on personality traits.

All I want to share is that nowadays, the attempt to pigeon-hole types or traits have ended up in a distorted version of the so-called healing sciences, including the treatment of personality disorders.

Personality disorders are classified into three main groups:

☼ the eccentric or paranoid,
☼ the emotional, anti-social or histrionic, or

☼ the anxious, associated with an obsessive and compulsive disorder.

This is the result of human behaviour. A hundred years ago, the child was taught manners by parents, relatives and society. The behaviour of the child was emphasized, so that his mental pattern was, in a way, restructured. The inner software of the mind's perception was changed by behaviour.

Today, we are trying the reverse viz. changing the mind by a special alteration of chemicals or drugs, in the hope that behaviour changes. Yet another imbalance! How can you dissociate the mental aspect from the behavioural side and vice versa?

You can affect a person's behaviour with repetition. The mental circuitry will acknowledge that this is a desirable behaviour due to the rewards given. A toddler's mother will reward him for good behaviour so the mind begins to set into realising that 'if I do this, if I give, if I am not too noisy, then, I will be rewarded, they will acknowledge me, they will clap for me, they will give me a gift, they will give me sweets'.

This brings us to the original key issue of the interplay between nature and nurture. Nature and nurture can never be separated. There are limitations and unchangeable aspects to each.

The rise of the West or the hegemony of the imperial Western culture that is dominating the world is based on the domestication of animals. They domesticated animals far earlier and more easily than others, especially the war animal, the horse. But there are numerous animals that cannot be domesticated, such as the many failed attempts to domesticate the zebra.

Nature has its limitations. You cannot, by nurturing alone, change a frog into a gecko. It cannot be! It requires dozens, maybe hundreds, of generations to tweak the genetic imprint.

Nature and nurture go together.

We all hope and pray to have inherited reasonable genes. We need to culture it and then nurture it.

But the right environment, the right teaching, the right methodology and the right mapping is also essential.

So, the process of grooming the self is

dependent on the combined influence of nature and nurture and hence, is impacted by your makeup, physically, materially, genetically, as well as culturally, and religiously. There is a limit though, as to how much can be influenced. Someone born with a disability or 'imbalance' can practise to make up for it; but there will always be a level of limitation.

We are all striving for perfection; perfection of our inner and outer relationship, our mind and heart, our behaviour and what we consider as our ethical values and standards, until we realise outwardly that we can never sustain anything that we consider to be perfect. That sustainability is beyond space and time. That sustainability is to do with the light in your heart. And only Allah is Ever-Perfect. You and I will strive all the time for a semblance of perfection in a particular context.

Imam Ali asked Prophet Muhammad to teach him his *sunnah*, the way of the Prophet, to which the Prophet is reported to have said:

> 'The *shari'ah* is my words, *tariqah*
> my actions, and *haqiqah* my state.
> Understanding is my capital, reason
> (*'aql*) the basis of my way of life (*din*),

and love my foundation; longing is
my mount, fear my companion, and
knowledge my weapon; forbearance is
my master, trust in Allah my helper, and
contentment my treasure; truthfulness
is my stopping place, certainty my
shelter, poverty my pride, and by it I
am honoured over all Prophets and
Messengers.'

This is the answer of an enlightened being
who possesses an inner knowledge based on his
witnessing!

Let us examine what the Prophet said. He
said that:

- Knowledge is his capital.

- Intellect or *'aql* and reason are the roots
  of his din (which has rationality and
  accountability).

- *Hub* or love is the foundation of his
  life, resonating with what Allah says in a
  hadith qudsi, 'I loved to be known.' We love
  the divine qualities, the divine character,
  His power, His immensity. That is why
  we try to emulate these qualities.

- The Prophet further replied that *Shawq* or enthusiasm (or passion) is his vehicle.

- *Dhikr* or awareness of the higher is his constant companion.

- Trust is his treasure. One must trust that Allah will show you. One must have total confidence that Allah will guide you. Is there any treasure greater than this? Is there any wealth higher than this?

The Prophet further stated that:

- Ilm or knowledge is his weapon.

- Patience is his cloak or garment.

- Contentment is the prize or his ultimate reward.

- Dependence on Allah is his pride.

- Zuhd or abstinence is his vocation.

- Certainty is his strength.

- Truth is his inner intercessor.

- Taa'ah or obedience is sufficient for him.

Now, if we try to enforce to any young person to be obedient, the question will be 'obedient to what?' So, they have to be taught and shown the map e.g. a youngster always wants to have everything for himself, but it will not work for long because he will end up having no friends. If you are like this nobody will be with you, so share your sweets. The child therefore begins to understand and accept obedience to the natural law of things and not just obedience to the father or mother.

Everybody wants success, from child to adult. But once they know the map, once they can read how everything fits together, they will naturally obey. Lower obedience is the characteristic of being humble, easy, having courage, being kind, not being angry all the time etc. These are the foundations.

When it comes to the *sunnah* there are between fifty to sixty terms that define the foundations, and another fifty or sixty terms and its opposites that define the higher aspirations. There are no less than thirty descriptions of emotions.

The basic emotions are considered to be six; amongst them is anger, bliss, fear and surprise, but the combinations bring about no less than thirty complex emotions, such as, to be self-aware and self-accountable – the things that you need to bear in mind if you are truly on the path of refining your character.

It is a complex map, but you need to start with the foundation, the basic sketches. Gradually develop and evolve until you are questioning the higher in you, questioning the light within the heart. Having already discussed it with others and taken counsel, you follow, as they say, your heart.

The Qur'an says:

> *'[To the righteous it will be said], "O reassured soul."'[89:27]*

Be careful and remember that you are not qualified, not self-sufficient. Allah reminds us:

> *'O you who have believed, repent to Allah with sincere repentance' [66:8]*

Return to Allah, call upon Allah and ask for the appropriate direction.

> *'...and when you have decided, then totally rely upon Allah. Indeed, Allah loves those who rely [upon Him]' [3:159]*

The definition of *tawaqqul* (total reliance) is a deep one. First you rely upon your *'aql* (intellect).

Then you rely upon people who are wiser than you. Then you rely upon the maker of it all, Allah. The Prophet advises to use your *'aql*, reason, and then trust in the higher. Notice this hierarchy of things.

> *'...and hold fast to Allah. He is your protector; and excellent is the protector, and excellent is the helper.' [22:78]*

Hold onto that rope: the rope of *iman* (faith based on trust) and *ihsan* (excellent or perfect conduct).

In this journey or passage there is movement, there is a changing of gear. You start by making *hijrah* (migration) and turning away from that which is not acceptable to you now. It may have been acceptable when you were a child, but with every year you are a different being. You are evolving from the lowest of 'me, me, me' to realising the light upon light upon light! *Hijra* and turning away is necessary!

From *hijrah* comes *jihad*, exerting energy. You must take a decision 'I will not do it! I won't do it! I will leave this place!' followed by appropriate, knowledgeable action. This will lead us to certainty. There is a hierarchy. You have to give up the lower and the higher will take over.

Allah reminds us in the Qur'an:

> '[The time of] their account has approached
> for the people, while they are in heedlessness
> turning away.' [21:1]

Accountability is close at hand, but we forget and postpone. Do you know if tomorrow will come for you? How do you know whether the air that goes in will come out? There is an urgency to exert ourselves, to be in *jihad* fully, in the inner and outer.

We remember, all the time, *Islam, Iman, Ihsan*. Islam is to submit to the truth that there is a hierarchy in me, that there is an animal in me and then, there is a light in me that can be higher than the angels.

The angels are limited. They cannot make mistakes, but I can. Allah has given me a trust that I can make mistakes and Allah has put in me this program 'that I will suffer'. But I do not want to suffer, so I have to take the divine offer. The pattern has already been set. The work is done. So, we have to drive on these multidimensional directions.

Our *din* is based almost entirely on obedience (the obedience after knowing) and following these templates and clear directions. The Prophetic teaching is that all is based on *tawbah* i.e. returning to Allah.

How do we return? By leaving your habit!

Remember and regret having wasted so much of your life. Then there is a need for *azam* and *tawakkul* (total reliance). Next comes *muraqaba* (reflection), followed by *muhasabah* (self-inventory).

Our actions are as good as our intentions. So, what is my *niyyah* (intention)? Is it just to make more money, to have more power or to be outwardly secure? What about my inner security? Ultimately I am an inner being. All is related to the meaning I give to life. All of it is based on *wafa* (faithfulness, loyalty), to be loyal to Allah, and *ikhlas* (sincerity). That is the meaning of *tarbiyah*. The Arabic root of tarbiyah is *Rabb* (Lord, Sustainer). Tarbiyah is 'to bring up' everyone to recognise the Lord who is Ever-Present.

The effort of constantly trying to correct

disorder from one direction only, rather than being accountable for one's behaviour, will not work. If you behave differently, then your mind will change. If the mind changes, the behaviour changes. The two are interlinked. We are both outer and inner; outer action and inner subtle feelings and intentions.

The ultimate goal of any refinement of character is to be as close as possible to the Prophetic model. We have beautiful descriptions of how the Prophet was. The Qur'an describes the Prophet:

> *'And indeed, you are of a great moral character'* [68:4].

The quality of the prophetic character is great. 'Great', as inconsistent and not subjected to the fluctuations of the outer world. When you have access to your Lord, to you Creator, to the light of Allah, nothing will ever disturb you other than responding appropriately.

A classical and famous description of the qualities of the Prophet is used by Imam Ghazali:

> 'He always helped with the house chores and he ate with the servants

and the family (meaning with the high
and the low, with the close ones and
with those who were not familiar). He
mended his sandals and he cared for
his mount. He milked the sheep. He
carried his shopping home. He shook
hands with the wealthy and the poor.
He never belittled a gift or turned down
any offer.'

Look at the *adab* (courtesy) of this magnificent being!

'He was easy to approach. He was
always pleasant. His disposition was
most attractive. He was generous, and
a good companion. He always had a
smile, but never laughed loudly. He was
concerned without a frown. He was
humble and accepting, being debased or
abased. He was soft-hearted and strong-
willed. He was always watching for what
is true. He was always reflective. He was
gentle with all his people. He was easy,
friendly with the young and the old.'

Another tradition tells us that *'he was honest, he*

was just, he was chaste and he had no waste'.

Consider how much we waste in this world!

'He ate what was available, sparingly and slowly. He visited the sick and attended funerals. He was silent without being insolent. He was eloquent without being lengthy.'

The Evolving Self

What are all the great traditions, especially the religious traditions of the Abrahamic line? These traditions are thousands of years old, started by this great being, the Prophet Ibrahim (AS), four thousand years before the advent of Isa (AS) and from it we are the ultimate heirs of the Islamic tradition.

What are *Islam*, *Iman* and *Ihsan*?

What is the ultimate state of realising that there is only the *nur* of Allah (which we recite constantly as *la ilaha illallah*)?

It is fine to say it with the tongue and understand it with the mind, but it is something else to be *transformed*. There must be The One from which all the dualities have come, and from Who all the pluralities have emanated.

Imam Ali said *'I didn't see a thing unless I saw Allah before it, I see Allah within it and I see Allah after it.'*

"I see" refers to seeing the unifying field... One, One, One.

From the One has come the twos and these dualities yearn to return to the One, to be able to make sense of things. At the end of time, at the end of the end, after *yawm al qiyamah*, there will again only be One.

The story of self-grooming, self-growth, self-evolvement and the refinement of character is to enable the realisation of both worldly and heavenly wisdom. Worldly wisdom requires dealing with cause and effect, rationality – 'is it the right time?', 'is it the right place?', 'are the people interested in these teachings?' Heavenly wisdom has its own logic and reasoning beyond worldly reason. It is said that 'the heart has a reason that reason knows not.' Everything in existence has its duality and its double.

> *'...Who created you from one soul and created from it its mate and dispersed from both of them many men and women'. [4:1]*

*'O you who have believed, remember Allah
with much remembrance'. [33:41]*

Remember Allah, remember the One.

Remember the origin.

Remember the essence.

Deal with the twos. Deal with the ups and downs, the good and the bad. Remember the One.

*'It is He who confers blessing upon you,
and His angels [ask Him to do so] that
He may bring you out from darknesses into
the light. And ever is He, to the believers,
Merciful.'[33:43]*

We come out from the darkness of confusion and ignorance to the *nur*, to the light of knowledge. Knowledge is so important!

First we have the intention. With the intention we need to get skills to acquire knowledge. There is no use having good intentions and being without knowledge. Then you act.

Intention

Skills

Knowledge

Actions

We need to reflect and develop a feedback system that asks, 'is it working?', 'is it beneficial?'

This enables you to participate in the world of change and its ups and downs, with the constant reference to that which never, ever changes – the light in your heart, the *nur* of Allah in us, His *ruh*.

> *'Say, Is it other than Allah I should take as a protector, Creator of the heavens and the earth' [6:14]*

Allah cracked (*fatara*) and opened up and caused this splitting of heavens and earth. *Fitrah* (primordial state, innate nature) is from the Arabic verb *fatara* which means to crack asunder, to open. It is the root of everything that has come into existence and has been created.

Fitrah also means to start, to begin. The verb is used when we refer to the earth splitting itself with greenery in spring. It is the original, innate, hidden software, *fatara*.

Numerous reminders in the Qur'an mention the primal state, visible and invisible, human and divine, that Allah put in the human beings:

*'So direct your face toward the religion,
inclining to truth. [Adhere to] the fitrah of
Allah upon which He has created [all] people.
No change should there be in the creation of
Allah. That is the correct religion, but most of
the people do not know.' [30:30]*

Fitrah is the essence of creation. What is the
nature of man? The *fitrah* is to do with the origin
of creation. It is the nature of man to be created
with both lows and highs.

*'And inspired it [with discernment of] its
wickedness and its righteousness' [91:8]*

This verse describes the *fitrah* from Allah
that 'inspires' human beings to have within them
the possibility of sinking low and rising high.

The creation of twos, doubles, and of many
multitudes is originally from one self. The one
self is the One *ruh*. Every one of us has this light
in our heart. All the things programmed come
from this light. Our duty is to groom ourselves
from the lower, to watch the lower tendencies.
Stop the lower and the higher is already there.
Our job is upbringing in *adab* (courtesy), in *akhlaq*
(refined conduct), in *suluk* (the refined behaviour

expected from the committed wayfarer on the path of enlightenment).

We are all animals; we are social creatures in need of society and community, and in need of people as mirrors, so that we rise higher and higher to the realisation of divine presence. This realisation gives us light-heartedness and illumination. Otherwise, we accuse and blame each other. Realise that no two moments are the same, no two animals are the same, and no two human beings are ever the same. And, if you do not refer to the higher within, you will remain divided.

Another meaning of *fitrah* is to be truly on the path:

> *'Indeed, I have turned my face toward He who created the heavens and the earth, inclining toward truth, and I am not of those who associate others with Allah'. [6:79]*

The seeker committed to *tawhid* (unity), to seeing the One, to being illumined by the light of the One, is the Prophetic being, the perfect being; he who has cracked, who has opened from nothing. It implies that the soul enables us to progress, according to the speed we can muster, towards the ever-presence of Allah. Our ritual practices are based on that. We do our *wudu'* (ablution), we separate from the world of differentiation, of ups and downs, so we can disappear into the realm of the Oneness through our *sajdah*.

Prostration is critical in our *din*.

The Prophet says the *salat* is the *miraj* of the believer. *Miraj* is flying up into the unknown heavens. If we are unable to disappear from this creation in our *salat*, then spiritually we have not recharged. You may have performed your obligatory *salat* as a ritual, but what about the inner nourishment?

The Qur'an says:

> '...and Allah has sealed over their hearts, so they do not know' [9:93]

This verse refers to a heart which is closed and frozen. If there is no love in our practice of the *din* it will not overflow. We suffer because we want to press upon others what we are used to in our own particular practices, but our hearts are closed – we do not have knowledge.

There is a big difference between knowledge and information. Our heritage is enriched with immense knowledge. Knowledge gives you inner certainty, inner contentment, inner joy. Take it away and all that remains is a ritual with no inner meaning.

Allah describes the creation:

'It is He who created the heavens and the earth in true (proportions): the day He saith, "Be", behold! It is. His word is the truth'. [6:73]

It is He who has created the heavens and earth by Truth. Truth is never-changing. *Haqq* never, ever changes. Everything else in life changes; it is relative. It is He who has created all the seen and unseen by the Absolute, by the Truth; there is only Truth. Everything else is trying to draw nourishment from the Truth, but it is transitory. It is short-lived. Everything has come and exists in according to a measure. It will pass. Every one of us, with every passing day, is closer to departure.

'...it is He who created all things, and ordered them in due proportions'. [25:2]

Everything is according to a measure.

'And Allah has created every animal from water...' *[24:45]*

Everything in existence has its opposite – good and bad, creation and death, day and night.

'And of every thing We have created pairs...'
                    [51:49]

'...that you may receive admonition' *[24:1]*

The word *tadhakkaroon* has a great meaning. It implies the moving beyond the twos and only remembering the One. The word *dhikr* is repeatedly used in the Qur'an challenging us to go beyond memory i.e. to go through the heart, to the knowledge that there is only One. This is the foundation of our *din*: In *la ilaaha illallah* is none other than the One, and in its echo *Muhammadan Rasoolullah*, there is multiplicity.

If the creation refers to the One, then life will be stable, there will be *barakah*, wholesomeness and goodness. If there is no reference to the One, then everyone has his own view and idea, and every brother is quarrelling with the next brother.

What is the human composition? Where is the primal nature or the natural disposition within us? We all want a healthy body, which is subjected to a mind of good quality and healthy attitude. Within man there is an important faculty called *'aql*, or intellect. Its main function is to contain and rein in the *nafs* by virtue of its reasoning and rationality. However, it can truly do this only with the *qalb*, the heart. The *qalb* is the higher and subtler foundation of the *'aql*. The *qalb* takes meaning to a higher dimension, based on love and submission.

The Qur'an repeatedly reminds us about the opening of the heart. It is not enough to only have a very highly developed and evolved intellect and reasoning. Many people have a very high IQ but they are not happy or content because they have not been living through the heart. The soul lies within the heart and the soul is God's light in us.

Connection with that light makes everything easier. Disconnection brings about difficulty and suffering. People are complaining, blaming and doing all the things we consider being human and normal; yet it is subhuman.

If human beings do not rise towards the purpose of their creation – to worship and adore

Allah – then they have missed the boat. Whether they miss the boat by one hour, one day or one year, it makes no difference. They have missed it and it has to do with *tawhid*, which is 'constant reference to the divine presence'.

What would the Prophet of Allah say if he were here? The answer requires from us the universality for which we have been designed and created. It will only come if the heart opens up to the different levels, one of which is witnessing – *shahid*-

'We have truly sent thee as a witness…'
[48:8]

Witness even if it is against you. If you have this silly inflated reputation about yourself, then you are already dead before you have died, because you do not accuse yourself. You accuse everybody else, except yourself, except your own ignorance. So, witness!

The Nature and Spectrum of the Self

There are many different ways of describing relationships and they all relate to each other.

Essentially relationships can be divided into three categories.

First, is 'the relationship with myself'.

Each one of us has the so-called 'you', a semi-independent or, at least, physically autonomous entity.

The question rises again 'who are you?' Are you this fellow who walks, sleeps, eats and dies and who is sometimes sick, sometimes happy or unhappy, sometimes facing difficulty or sometimes facing ease? And we are all the same regarding this. Every human being has been confronted with difficulties and ease, with insecurity and security, with being appreciated and unappreciated, with being respected and disrespected. We all have been subjected to these different states. The relationship within myself is an essential one. Also, the relationship within my *self* is ever-changing – this is my conditioned consciousness – it never stops from babyhood until the grave.

But, the relationship of consciousness to pure consciousness (my soul), which is within my heart, does not change. This relationship allows us constant improvement of behaviour; if I refer to the inner in me I become more patient, less dogmatic and more tolerant.

We have numerous teachings about this relationship from the Qur'an, the *sunnah* and the *sirah* of the Prophet.

> *'By the Soul, and the proportion and order given to it; And its enlightenment as to its wrong and its right.' [91:7-8]*

The *nafs*, the self, has within it *fujoor* i.e. decadence and corruption; and it also has *taqwa* i.e. obedience and steadiness. Therefore I can be mean, I can be greedy and I can also be modest. I can have fear and I can also have courage. I can be unreasonable and I can also be logical, rational and reasonable. I can be dictatorial and I can also be just.

The Prophet teaches us to 'speak and apply justice even when it is mostly against you'. Charity begins at home. Fairness is required. A society that acknowledges fair play lasts longer, and develops. On the other hand, a society that uses oppression and depression does not grow and evolve.

The relationship between my lower self and higher self is essential. If the *nafs (lower self)* fulfils its obligation to evolve towards the knowledge of its One Source, then it reflects Allah's plan for all of us; it reflects our *fitrah*. If, however, it has been distorted as a reflector, then it takes on the myriad of forms that are classified below:

The Commanding Self – Nafs al-ammara

If the *nafs* is completely wayward and has lost touch with its *fitrah*, it is classified as *nafs al-ammara*. This is the totally selfish, most egotistical of the selves which, as the Qur'an says, 'commands to evil' [12:53]. It is the self of the self-centred three-year old child or the despot who wants something and wants it instantly. This *nafs* will not listen to reason or rationality.

The Blaming Self – Nafs al-lawwama

Slightly higher on the scale is the *nafs* whose conscience is pricked because of its bad behaviour. As a result, it blames itself for being extreme and may be spurred into positive action in order to do something about its dismal condition.

The Inspired Self – Nafs al-mulhama

If the *nafs al-lawwama* progresses further along the path, improving itself, becoming more tolerant and inspired, perhaps even creative, it becomes what is known as *nafs al-mulhama* i.e. the inspired self. It says 'why not?' or 'It's crazy, let's do it!' Everything goes, even the wildest ideas.

The Certain Self – Nafs al-mutma'inna

When the *nafs* is brought under control, it is on the road to contentment, to becoming *nafs al-mutma'inna*. This self is certain that with diligence, commitment, honesty, companionship and applying the right prescriptions it will come to faithfully reflect the *fitrah*. It will increase in its certainty that it has come from beyond time; that it is only here to learn, to experience and to be poised for that final, incredible journey.

The relationship between the *nafs*, the lower self, and the higher self is essential because it leads the created entity, the 'I', to the Creator via the agency of the soul.

With frequent reference to the higher within me, the light in my heart becomes my first guideline. Purification of the heart is important because the soul resides in the spiritual heart within each one of us. We need to have a reasonably healthy body, a healthy mind and then a pure heart.

A pure heart means no rancour, no anger, no hatred, nothing. The relationship between myself to my Self is the starting point of childhood in spiritual growth. The second aspect is the relationship with others. We are distinguished from most other animals by the fact that we cannot grow, survive or evolve unless we are part of a society. The society is mirroring us. We love being with like-minded, like-hearted people. We end up having cultures, races and languages. The human civilization shows that we prefer what we are familiar with.

We have all kinds of clans, tribes and

nations. The Western evolvement seems to have dominated the rest of the world. In this model it is the nation unit that brings a clearly defined identity. Only a nation can be a so-called 'state', from a political perspective.

The 'relationship with others' is essential. Look at the development of a baby. In the early stages it begins with others. The first few months the baby needs none other than the mother. The seeds of qualities, such as trust, are planted in the baby. And we have all come across people who are mistrustful or distrusting. They do not have faith. Faith is not their guideline.

For them, the feeling of faith was probably not brought about in early life. If the cry of a baby is not attended to, how can there be trust in anything or anyone? The cry is an expression of disturbance and disturbance is life itself. If a child does not play, gurgle or drool, it is a very frightening thing for the mother. A mother wants a reaction from her child, which is a disturbance. Gradually the baby learns how to cope with the disturbances until such time when she becomes 'independent'…'She owns her own apartment'. What does 'independent' mean?

From the early stages of babyhood, the seeds of the higher attributes are planted in us. If you had it smooth as a baby, then you become accustomed to a positive attitude like

'I don't know what to do, but I will know what to do in a bit of time'. In other words, you do not become flustered. You have faith and trust. You have the notion that things will change, that it will be alright. It is not all gloomy.

The biography of growth and development in terms of relationships soon leads us into relating to the uncle, the aunt, the visitors and the others and then you start differentiating – this is an outsider, this is an insider, this is a family member, this is somebody who does not know our *din*, etc.

The relationship with others is a very important aspect of the normal growth of human beings, until you reach the realisation that in truth there is no otherness. Our *din* has numerous teachings about different nations. In truth we are the sons of *Bani Adam*. All of us are the same. We all want peace, tranquility, goodness, ease and comfort so that we can transcend the limitations of the body, mind and all of the other limitations we are subjected to. We desire the so-called freedom. Freedom starts with the freedom of expression, freedom from needs, from hunger, from pain. Ultimately, free from what? Freedom from one's self, and freedom from otherness.

In truth, other-ness is an obstacle.

'Nor can goodness and evil be equal. Repel (evil) with what is better: Then will he between whom and thee was hatred become as it were thy friend and intimate!' [41:34]

Face the enemy; think he is your friend with no enmity, anger or rancour in your heart. This illumined state comes when we follow the path prescribed in our *din*:

'Those who believed, and adopted exile, and fought for the Faith, with their property and their persons, in the cause of Allah...' [8:72]

Look at the perfection of layer after layer! First you have faith that you will come to know that you will not only be informed but also be transformed. Then *hajaroo* i.e. you leave behind that which is unacceptable, maybe also physical *hijrah*; and greater than that is *hijrah* from that which you love and want to keep. Then you exert your *jihad* i.e. you do your best outwardly and inwardly to move away from that which is keeping you in the animal state.

We are reminded:

'O you who have believed! Why do you say that which you do not do?' [61:2]

Those who have some faith, why do you say things that you don't do? Why don't you connect your word, your intention, and your verbal skills with your physical deeds? The din is based on *tawhid*. If you do not unify your thoughts, intentions and actions, how can you talk about subtler aspects of *tawhid*?

Allah promises:

'And those who strive in Our (cause), – We will certainly guide them to our Paths: For verily Allah is with those who do right.' [29:69]

The serious seekers and believers, who truly struggle on this path to discover the truth behind the multitudes of shadows, will certainly be guided on the right ways.

Our *din* is *mu'aamilah*, a relationship; a relationship between myself, within my heart, with others, with society, with humanity, with the trees and nature. We inherited enormous amounts of teachings regarding the human relationship to the environment, many of them regarding our relationship with the plant kingdom and the animal kingdom. We cannot just kill, eat, live and cut trees. As civil people we are concerned with the current situation. Part of the problem is because the leadership of our history was not Prophetic. Most of the Muslim situations continued in a rebellious way. We cannot accept this because it does not relate to the Prophet's way.

The issue of relationships involves personal responsibility, immediate responsibility right here and now, until we discover that *Islam* (submitting to the Truth) will lead us to faith, *Iman*. We will discover faith based on trust if we struggle and follow the path sufficiently until we see the connection to *Ihsan* (perfect conduct).

Allah is the *muhsin*. One of Allah's names – *al-Muhsin* – is He who gives unconditionally, out of love. If we want to access a bit of that closeness, we too must occasionally give unconditionally. Give conditionally also! That is also very good. It is a transaction…

'I'll give that if you do this'. But what about a higher element? Remember that Allah gives even to all his enemies. If we are truly on the path of Truth, *haqq*, we too must occasionally give charity without any expectations or conditions. It is not very easy.

The third aspect of relationships, and the most important, is the relationship between each one of us, to the *ruh*, to Allah, to the light of Allah.

There are many classifications of how the enormous, amazing light of Allah created all that we know and do not know.

Personality and Conduct

The *raqib* is the monitoring self. It asks: 'Is it the right place? Is it the right time? Is it the right context?' This is very challenging. One needs discipline to understand the right context, the right place, the right attitude. One can grow in age, but not in wisdom. Wisdom, worldly wisdom, is to call upon the *raqib* in you.

From *raqib* comes the *karim*. Essentially the

karim is the real 'I'. Maybe I can hide who I am (not show our real intentions, our inner side), but our cells *know* and have a record. Every cell within us has in it the story of the entire creation that we represent.

The Inner Senses

Just as there are five outer senses, there are also **five inner senses.** The first of the inner senses is termed *combining sense,* known in Arabic as *al-hiss al-mushtarak.* It combines the outer senses so that we relate together our abilities to hear and touch and so on, to gain a complete sensory picture of the outer world, in our minds.

The second inner sense is the faculty of *khayal* often translated as imagination. *Khayl* enables us to imagine different forms and formats of things and to place them in different contexts. *Khayl* is derived from the Arabic root word, *khayl* which means 'horse', and it is so named because of the effect generated by a herd of horses as they gallop. To onlookers, it seems as if the horses undulate and shimmer as their shiny coats catch the light of the sun, similar to the way in which images flicker through our minds.

The third inner sense is called the *wahima,*

which enables us to give value to forms and attributes. The *wahima* has to be flexible as situations change; a one-time friend may become an enemy, and vice versa.

The fourth faculty is *hafiza*, the faculty of memory. It is the storehouse of images and experiences from our past to which we have immediate access. We all have memories which are related to the outer senses and to our emotions.

The last inner sense is called *mufakkira*. This is the faculty of cognition or thinking. This faculty can take us from where we are to the unseen zones, with the *'aql* and the *qalb* working together. Fikr is a related word meaning reflection, meditation, contemplation.

The main purpose of the inner faculties is to help us relate to our constantly changing world. If our common sense is in a healthy state, our faculty of imagination is reliable, our ability to place values on forms is sound and flexible and our reservoir of information and memories from the past is constantly updated, we may then reflect in an efficient manner.

We need reflection; we are in need of

reference to what brings us close to the reflection of Truth. Truth does not change. Everything else does!

We all have memory. The more the memory is revised, the more dynamic is the *'aql*, the mind, and the healthier is the brain, which is the seat of the mind. Everything is taking place within the brain. How does it happen? We can discern the chemical changes, the physiological changes, the physical changes, the electromagnetic changes. But we do not know how it is translated into action. Another mystery!

In the process of grooming the self, 'changing your attitude, and changing your behaviour' is key. We can equally say 'change the mind'. Change the mind now and you will be saved from your fears and anxieties. The mind in us, an innate gift from Allah, enables us to live a life of ease if we allow it to flow. Allow the inner drive to show us that some of the things we want or don't want are not necessarily going to lead us to the higher position that we aim for (the higher position meaning access to the highest within us). Take that access to the highest in us away and most things become drudgery and distraction.

'I want to do good things' – it is good to do good things. It is good to build a mosque, but have you discovered the mosque within? Have you discovered the light of Allah in the heart? If not, we end up trying to impinge upon others and give a lot of discourses. If it does not come from the heart, and it does not touch hearts, we have not done it! Mere preaching is useless as it repeats the same old thing.

The young and the educated people do not want it. They want transformation; and it doesn't happen when we separate the spiritual aspect of our *din* from the religious aspect. In truth, they are never separated. They are ever-connected.

Our *din* connects heavens and earth, connects this earthy human being to the possibility that is beyond angels, as Adam was. If we separate them, we end up having rituals without the transformation – a lot of information with little transformation.

Refinement of character implies correct outward conduct, accountable to *shari'ah*. This is the essence of *Madinah*. However, do not forget that you were created for *Makkah*, towards the house of God. Without *Makkah*, *Madinah* becomes a lot of quarrels. *Makkah* without *Madinah* is not complete because we want society and we need community. Put the two together (*Makkah* and *Madinah*) and you are on the *Muhammadi* path!

When discussing upbringing or grooming of the self, the essential thing to realise is the dynamics of opposites – good and bad, vice and virtue. In life we experience both. You can never go through life without the opportunity and the grace of experiencing good and bad, acceptable and unacceptable, healthy and unhealthy, friend and enemy. And it goes from one end of the spectrum to the other.

The *nafs* is described in the Qur'an:

> *"By the Soul, and the proportion and order given to it"* [91:7]

Allah is describing to us this strange beast, the human being and his composition.

> *'And its enlightenment as to its wrong and its right'* [91:8]

Fujooraha means decadence, disruption, and breakdown. And it's opposite is *taqwa*, which is

integration, wellness, awareness. It is cautious
awareness and concern.

'Truly he succeeds that purifies it' [91:9]

Here is the key word, he who has brought
tazkiyah to his self has won, is victorious… He
who has brought *zakat* – what is the word *zakat*?
The Arabic word *za-kaf-ya* means to purify. The
zakat is obligatory upon all Muslims. It implies
that because we all love wealth, we all love money
and we all love power, then, by giving a portion
of it, we are reducing our attachment, our lust,
our greed and our love for it.

The *ayah* says he who purifies himself, he
who is intent to transcend the self, is winning
Aflaha Hayya 'alal-falah. Falah implies turning
things upside-down. In Arabic fallaah means
peasant because he turns the earth in order to get
rid of the weeds and give some air and newness.

But, elsewhere it is mentioned in the Qur'an
'do not ever think you can purify your lower *nafs*.'

'Therefore ascribe not purity unto yourselves.'
[53:32]

How do we reconcile these two ayat?

One says 'he who purifies it will win' and the

other *ayah* says 'do not ever think you will be able to purify your *nafs*'. The Qur'an uses the word *nafs* in a broad sense. The first reference is to *insan* in general. It is not about the lower self; it is about the *middle* self. It is talking about 'you and I'. Sometimes we are generous, other times we are mean, we are happy, we are unhappy, up and down like most human beings. The *ayah* implies that he who remains aware of the lower self, or of shaytan within, will win.

The second *ayah* implies 'do not ever think you will get rid of your lower self.' So, just turn away from it. Cover it up. Ask for Allah's merciful 'cover' by saying *Astaghfiru'llah*! Apologise, be humble. Do not ever think you will not have the lower greedy, meanness within you. The meaning reads 'Do not ever think you will be rid of it', because, if you get rid of it, you will not exist in this body; and we love the body and are in need of it.

In the first seven or eight years, the child only knows the body. Later on we begin to learn about the body and the mind. If, by the time we reach our forties or fifties, we don't realise the eternal light within us, then we are miserably imprisoned. We have not finished the job. The job, to begin with, is to be egotistic and mean. It is to be a child…pinching, concealing, lying and accusing others (everybody is at fault). But when you are in your fifties and sixties, and if you have not discovered that every fault is from you, then you have missed it. You are going to miss it all.

Everything we experience is only by Allah's grace. Everything in its engine, is suspended by the truth. A *lie* is the *covering* of the truth. A small lie is allowing a little of the truth to emerge:

> *'He to whom belongs the dominion of the*
> *heavens and the earth: no son has He begotten,*
> *nor has He a partner in His dominion: it is*
> *He who created all things, and ordered them in*
> *due proportions.' [25:2]*

There is measure to everything. Nothing ever exists in this world unless it has a quality and a quantity. Quantity is a measure and quality is an attribute. We ask 'is it acceptable to Allah'? 'Is it going to liberate us from the lower self or is it going to increase that inner fire?'

Allah describes it in the Qur'an:

> *'…one whom the Evil one by his touch Hath*

driven to madness…' [2:275]

The people who this verse relates to are hit from all sides. They do not know when they are going to fix the currency exchange or get more wealth. We love to increase until we live in the grave. To increase what? A bit of this and a bit more of that until you don't know where to put the stuff anymore. The only sustainable increase is the orientation towards the inner light; Allah's light, through sharing and caring for others. We are trapped in this miserable little prison if we have not found the way of redemption from the lower self.

'…and in all that Allah hath created, in the heavens and the earth, are signs for those who fear Him' [10:6].

There are 16 or 17 *ayat* saying that all the signs are great lessons for those who know. They are lessons to know the differentiation between the lower self, the material, worldly issues, human life, and the light and eternity.

The Prophetic descriptions of this *'ilm* (knowledge) are numerous. We have to put things in the right place, not haphazardly. For example:

- If you have a toothache you have to address the cause and the effect. It is not a superstition or a higher thing. The toothache is a warning to correct something before it worsens. . It is causal and relates to the mind.

- Become emotional and you are disturbing the heart, which represents the access to your soul. Through the soul you perceive the appropriateness of knowledge.

Classifications of the Self

There is a basic system of classifying the self as consisting of three levels or aspects viz. the vegetal self, the animal self and the rational self.

In life, the first phase that the self encounters concerns the act of feeding, which is followed by growth and development and eventually by reproduction. The next phase of the self is concerned with sensing and movement, and this is followed by the third phase of knowledge and discrimination. Within each of these phases there is an awareness of perfection inherent within the soul, which carries it towards its fullest potential.

The Vegetal Self

The vegetal self has three faculties or powers, namely, the powers of *feeding, growth and reproduction.*

The first power is that of feeding which fashions an entity into one of its own species. The second is the power of growth itself, to grow in proportionate measure to its own kind. The third is that of reproduction through a seed giving rise to a new cycle.

The Animal Self

The animal self has, in addition to the faculties of the vegetal self, the additional powers of *comprehension and movement.* The power of comprehension is to interpret and apprehend information from the outside world through the five inner senses. The faculty of movement enables the entity to be able to transport itself according to its will. Although the vegetal self has a degree of mobility, its movement does not occur by will, since it is devoid of conscious will.

Mobility arises from two sources: the first is by direct power of action, such as moving a limb or an appendage. The second source is from the cause behind the action, that is, its intention. This primary motive has to do with yearning or desire. The motivation to move arises from the desire to obtain something that is wanted. This motivation in turn is based on the faculty of imagination, for when an image or a thought of what is desirable or repulsive occurs in the imagination, that image gives rise to a motive to move either forward or back, whereupon movement ensues.

So, the animal self is drawn towards what the faculty of imagination deems to be desirable and necessary, and is repulsed by what it imagines to be undesirable and destructive. This dynamic of attraction and repulsion is fundamental to all creation. The power of attraction and the power of repulsion are the two basic motivating factors in life.

The Rational Self

As the third and the highest level of the self, the rational self possesses all the qualities of the vegetal self and the animal self, and it has the power of *action or doing and the power of knowledge.*

The power of action is the power by which the body is protected, nourished and raised to its full maturity, and by which the self is able to overcome its lower animalistic tendencies. As for the power of knowing, it can view matters and processes in theory and abstraction. It refers back constantly to the faculty of memory to maintain its connection to the origin of all its actions.

So the journey of the self begins from the lowest stage of its vegetal aspect and evolves towards its highest stage until it reaches the objective for which it was created.

The cosmological plan briefly explains the creation by successive emanation of worlds:

Alam-i-Hahut (Realm of Oneness): The Realm of pre-existence, the condition of the universe before its formation, equated with the unknowable essence of God.

Alam-i-Lahut (Realm of Divinity): The world where incalculable unseen tiny dots emerge and expand to large circles that they engulf the entire universe. It is the realm of Allah's attributes.

Alam-i-Jabarut (Realm of Power): The universe is constituted into features.

Alam-i-Malakut (Angelic Realm): The characteristics of the species and their individuals descend from the Realm of omnipotence and separate consciousnesses comes into being.

Alam-i-Nasut (Realm of Humans): The foundations of the tangible world of matter are laid. It encompasses the material realm and all the visible cosmos.

The Realm of Oneness, *Hahut*, cannot be described.

The Prophet advises us to only discuss Allah's attributes, which is the second emanation, *Lahut*.

The Realm of Power, *Jabarut*, is the origin of the *arwah* – angels and jinn.

The Angelic Realm, *Malakut* is neighbouring the earth and is often referred to as the angelic realm.

The earthiness is *Mulk*; it has cause and effect, give and take, up and down, reason. Everything is glorifying and praising Allah and His qualities. Human beings love all Allah's attributes e.g. the Ever-Lasting, the Ever-Powerful, *al-Warith* (He who inherits everything). Some unhappy young people with wealthy parents pray that they 'may leave soon', so they become the *warith*. One day they are too going to leave the wealth behind. At best we are custodians.

For a spiritual seeker the journey in this life represents a constant movement from the material realm towards the subtle zone of the unseen that lies beyond our comprehension. It is a journey which begins with self-awareness and ends with soul-realisation. That is the real purpose and path of liberation from all limitations.

> *'Hasten ye then (at once) to Allah: I am from Him a Warner to you, clear and open!'*
> *[51:50]*

Run hastily to Allah. Return to Allah. Supplicate to Allah.

So, we humble ourselves. We are reminded that our limited minds cannot contain nor define Allah; 'if Allah is enough for you, then everything is enough for you'! It suffices to know that all is under His governance and His control!

A constant reminder for all the *arwah* in our hearts is:

> *'Am I not your Lord (who cherishes and sustains you)?'* *[7:172]*

This is the golden thread of *tawhid* and the foundation of our *din*! It permeates every known and unknown situation, every aspect of creation, seen or unseen.

The foundation of all relationships is *The One*, Allah, from Whom cascaded an overflowing of *Rahmah* as multitudes of layers of shadows and lights. This is our heritage. We do not denounce anything that exists, but refer it, all the time, to the Source of all existence and creation, Allah.

Relationships

Numerous experiments show that we are more than homo-economicus.

The famous 'Ultimatum Game' is a game used by the departments of psychology and sociology. The rule of the game states that if I give you something and tell you to share it with someone else, you can share it if both of you are happy with the share portions. If either one of you is unhappy, you don't receive anything. The results showed a cut-off point of 20%.

For example, if I give you R100, and you give the other player R20, keeping R80 for yourself, he may accept. But if you give him only R5 and you keep R95, he will seek 'revenge'. Yet, rationally, as per the homo-economicus principle, to get R5 is better than nothing. So, despite the 'rationality' of R5 being better than zero, the sense of justice in us, inspired by the soul, will not allow it. And Allah is The Just, al-'Adl.

The different layers of the self will judge the situation. *Nafs al-mulhamah*, the inspired self says 'share a bit'. *Nafs al-mutma'innah*, the certain self, says 'I am certain I will come to know, provided I do the right exercises to attain knowledge, like abandonment of nonsense, greed, fantasy, illusion and backbiting'.

There is interplay between quality and quantity. If you improve quality, and reduce the quantity, you will only see the light of One. *Nafs al-radiyah*, the contented self, inspires you to be an *'Abd Allah'*, a servant of Allah, because no longer are you a slave of your own whims.

We want to attract goodness, whether it is money, acknowledgement, admiration or love. The force of attraction makes us beasts. The force of repulsion or anger (shouting, accusing others) makes us predatory. These are vices. With refinement I come to realise that I can groom myself and this leads one to decide 'I don't want everything to myself'. This 'modesty' is associated with chastity, tranquility, patience, liberality, integrity, sobriety, the zeal to accomplish good, self-discipline, good disposition, steadiness and piety.

Every virtue is like a dot because it is specific and perfect. The vices are around that dot. The example of self-control (to be patient) is a great virtue. It is surrounded by excesses like lack of restraint and impatience. Impatience is endless while patience is not. Patience is a specific point where time stops. And, *As-Sabur* is Allah's name.

Virtue may be defined as that mode of behaviour that falls between two extremes of vices. We have to be careful when talking about piety and generosity. The Prophet says 'he who thinks or is aware of his piety is worse than he who is not pious'. It is subtle... for 'don't you know who I am? I am a very good person'. So, if you only see 'the good person' in you, then you miss the light of He who has created all persons. And it becomes more subtle and more dangerous as you progress along the path of self-knowledge.

The forces of repulsion are also known as the forces of anger. When this power is in equilibrium in relation to its opposite qualities of 'fight' on the one extreme and 'flight' on the other, the virtue of courage emerges.

Used wisely, the vices may become stepping stones or keys to virtues. From the virtue of courage comes greatness of spirit, confidence, fortitude, self-control. The virtue of courage lies between the two vices of recklessness and cowardice.

All the spiritual practices in our *din* are based on 'turning away' from the negative behaviour. We resent these negative behaviours and ask Allah for cover or forgiveness by saying *Astaghfiru'llah*. We may be religious in our old age, but the lifelong grooming of our character is essential. Are we ready and content to leave this world joyfully? The Prophet reminded us that 'we die as we lived'. Imam Ali says 'if you want to know whether an action is right, and that it is not going to increase your ego, think of yourself dying with that action'.

Watch out! The air that goes in may not come out.

The person ready to leave this world at any moment is reasonably qualified to have the world under his feet. If not, it is on top of his head! The back begins to bend. The chest has not been cleared. He is not *'Abd Allah* (servant of Allah) and certainly not the guest of Allah!

The rational self, evolves when it follows the path of divine guidance. As a result of this obedience and submission to the Light, it attains the ultimate virtue of wisdom and knowledge. Wisdom gives the self, access to the knowledge of 'the divine' and 'the human'. It also provides the self with discrimination between wrong and right. People become trustworthy!

When the three high virtues of wisdom, courage and modesty combine in the self the result is the highest virtue of all, justice.

Justice makes the self, behave fairly – to itself and to others. The just man is impartial, giving to others what is equally useful for himself. The just man is rational and open to criticism, not blaming others. There is injustice everywhere in the world because of our actions. If we don't put 'number one' right, then the 'One and only One' will not show us His ultimate wisdom. Then we deserve the suffering, so that we may turn away from individual and collective misery, towards the ever-present divine offering.

The virtues that arise from justice are

friendship, harmony, fellowship, honest dealing, fair play, amicability and devotion.

In conclusion, remember the foundational pillars of our *din*:

1. *Hijrah* (emigration) – move away from that which is not acceptable; turn away; leave false security behind. Be ready to leave this world.

2. With it comes *Jihad*, expending energy. Do whatever you can. And, in our case, we are sharing the inner meaning of our *din*, the transformative aspect of this great package of *'Islam, Iman, Ihsan'*.

3. *'Amal*, action. Do it! Whether by your limbs or by your tongue. Act according to what is in your heart. Otherwise, we become hypocrites.

4. Knowledge is the result of action. Knowledge leads us to *yaqin*, certainty that Allah is guiding us. Allah guides and helps the believer who is certain and trusting that there is security in the eternal light. These are Allah's signs. The Qur'an is the book of signs, the book

of *ayat*. These are signs within the hearts of those who have knowledge. What is the source of it? It is the *ruh* inside our heart. We take reference from our original *fitrah*, and not from our personal history encumbered by memory and experiences.

This *ayah* resolves it:

'...and never give up hope of Allah's Soothing Mercy: truly no one despairs of Allah's Soothing Mercy, except those who have no faith.' [12:87]

Trust the divine light, the *ruh* of Allah, the essence of Allah behind all of creation. Turn away from darkness. Light is already there.

Vices and suffering are the way of this kindergarten called 'earth', to turn you towards virtues and the divine offering that is ever-present.

May Allah enable us to pursue this path of ever-grooming our self and ever-turning away from our negativity towards good qualities, the colours of Allah, the qualities of Allah!

Glossary

'Abd Allah (pl. 'ibad Allah)	Servant of Allah
Adab	Courtesy
'Adl / 'adalah	Justice / fairness
Akhira	The hereafter or eternal life
Akhlaq	Refined conduct
Al-'Alim	The All Knowing. One whose knowledge is infinite
Al-Akhir	The Last
Al-Awwal	The First

Al-Azim	The Magnificent
Al-Baqi	The Everlasting
Al-Ghani	The Rich beyond need
Al-Haqq	The Absolute Truth
'Alim	Learned, knowledgeable; a scholar
Al-Karim	The Most Generous
Al-Muhsin	He who gives unconditionally, out of love
Al-Qawi	The Most Strong
'Amal	Action
'Aql	Faculty of intellectual perception, from 'aqala, to realise, understand
Ar-Razzaq	The Ever Providing

As-Sabur The Patient

Al-Warith He who inherits everything

Astaghfiru'llah Asking Allah for the cover of forgiveness

Ayah A sign, more specifically a verse or sentence from the Qur'an; pl. ayat

'Ayn al-yaqin The eye of certainty

Din The life-transaction of Islam; from *dana* to owe or to be indebted to

Dhikr Remembrance or invocation of Allah

Dunya The temporal world and its concerns and possessions

Fitrah   Original nature of man,
                    deeply imprinted within
                    him, from *fatara*, to split or
                    cleave, break apart (hence
                    futur, fast-breaking), to bring
                    into being

Fiqh   Jurisprudence, the science
                    of deriving laws in keeping
                    with the essence of Islam,
                    from *faqiha*, to comprehend
                    or have knowledge of
                    something

Hadith   Tradition from the Prophet,
                    from *haddatha*, to relate
                    or report and *hadatha*, to
                    happen or to occur

Hadith qudsi   Sacred tradition, i.e. from
                    Allah via the tongue of the
                    Prophet

Hajj   Pilgrimage to Makkah

Hahut	Boundless, Essential Oneness of God. Derived from the Divine Name *Huwa*, 'He', and formed by analogy with the following terms, here given in descending hierarchical order: *Lahut* (the Divine, Creative Nature); *Jabarut* (the Divine Power or Immensity, the world form); *Malakut* (the Kingdom of the angels, the spiritual world); *Nasut* or *Mulk* (human nature, and in particular man's bodily form)
Haqq	Truth, reality; al-Haqq (Divine name)
'Haqq al-yaqin	Truth of certainty
'Haqq al-haqq	The Truth of Truth
Hayat	Life

Hijrah	Emigration
Ihsan	Excellent or perfect conduct
Ikhlas	Sincerity
'Ilm	Knowledge
'Ilm al-yaqin	Knowledge of certainty. Intellectual understanding and appreciation of an event. The first level of awareness of an event.
Iman	Faith based on knowledge. It is not blind belief.
Insan	Man, mankind
Insal al-Kamil	The perfected being
Islam	Submission; from *aslama* yielding to reality, obedience, purity and peace

Jihad	Struggling or striving for the sake of Allah; from *jahuda* to exert one's utmost
Khalifah	Vicegerent or steward; he who stands in the place of
Kitab	Book, the Qur'an
La illaha illa'llah	There is no god but Allah
Manazil'u sa'ireen	The spiritual stations of the wayfarer
Ma'rifah	Gnosis, enlightenment
Madinah	The town of Yathrib renamed after the Prophet and his followers emigrated there; first Muslim city
Makkah	The ancient town of Bakkah, home of the Ka'bah

Mi'raj	Night of Ascension, or Night Journey, specifically of the Prophet, but symbolically and potentially of every worshipper who prays sincerely ('The prayer of the believer is his Night Ascension' – the Prophet
Muhsin	One who acts and behaves in the best and most appropriate way
Nafs	The self, the ego
al-Nafs al-ammarah	The lower self which commands to evil. It is the lowest aspect of the human ego, but above the vegetal, mineral and animal
al-Nafs al-lawwamah	The critical or reproachful self

al-Nafs al-mardiyah	The self that is pleasing to Allah. At this level self and soul are in alignment
al-Nafs al-mulhamah	The inspired self
al-Nafs al-mutma'innah	The reconciled or tranquil self
al-Nafs al-radiyah	The contented self
Niyyah	Intention; the essential and first part of any act of worship, or indeed undertaking
Nur	Light
Qalb	Heart
Qur'an	Book revealed by Allah to the Prophet Muhammad (S)
Rahma	Merciful, a divine key attribute of Allah

Raqib	The monitoring self
Ruh	Soul, breath of life (pl. *arwah*). From *raha*, to do anything in the evening or at sunset, to go away, and *rawwaha*, to refresh, animate. *Ruh* is spirit, which is subtle, while *nafs* is self, which is rigid
Sajdah	The prostration of prayer in which one's self is obliterated in the glorification of Allah
Salat	Prayer; the prescribed form of prayer in Islam
Sawm	Fasting
Shahid	Witness
Shari'ah	Revealed code of conduct and law

Sibghat Allah   The ' colour' of Allah

Sirah   Life or biography of the
Prophet (S)

Suluk   The refined behaviour
expected from the
committed wayfarer on the
path of enlightenment

Sunnah   Custom or life pattern,
usually in reference to the
Prophet Muhammad (S),
but also in reference to
Allah

Taba'   To print, to press, to re-
produce; *matba'a* is printing
press

Taqwa   Cautious or fearful
awareness; God
consciousness

Tarbiyah   Grooming, raising; the
                    process by which a child
                    is brought up to realise his
                    inner potential as 'abd Allah

Tariqah   Path, literally 'way' of
                    the committed seeker of
                    enlightenment. A term also
                    used in Sufi brotherhoods

Tawhid   Unity, the Oneness of Allah

Tawakkul   Total reliance

Tawbah   Return/repentance

Wali   Saint, also governor in
                    modern Arabic

Wudu'   Ritual ablution involving
                    washing the face, forearms
                    and feet to consecrate
                    the self before prayer.
                    The Prophet advocated
                    maintaining a constant state
                    of *wudu'*

Yaqin	Certainty
Zakat	Obligatory wealth tax
Zuhd	Abstention, frugality, or doing without

www.ingramcontent.com/pod-product-compliance
Lightning Source LLC
Chambersburg PA
CBHW032046040426
42449CB00007B/1010